CHARLES T. GRIFFES

PIECES FOR CHILDREN

*The songs in this collection were previously published by
G. Schirmer, Inc. under the pseudonym of Arthur Tomlinson.*

ED-3918

ISBN 978-0-7935-3539-2

G. SCHIRMER, Inc.

DISTRIBUTED BY

HAL•LEONARD®
CORPORATION
7777 W. BLUEMOUND RD. P.O. BOX 13819 MILWAUKEE, WI 53213

It seems that, one day in 1918, Charles Tomlinson Griffes walked into G. Schirmer's Music Store in New York City looking for some "decent" piano pieces for beginners. He needed them for his work at the Hackley School in Tarrytown, where one of his responsibilities was teaching piano. After spending considerable time looking through Schirmer's inventory, Griffes complained that he couldn't find anything suitable for his students. Someone at Schirmer suggested that if Griffes couldn't find anything he liked, why didn't he write some beginner's pieces himself? He promptly did. Schirmer, who had published many songs and piano compositions by Griffes beginning in 1909, liked the pieces well enough to offer to publish them. Griffes was delighted with the opportunity and sold the *Six Short Pieces*, *Six Patriotic Songs*, and *Six Bugle-Song Pieces* outright to Schirmer in April and May 1918 for a total of $290.00 (comparable to about $2,700.00 in 1994). They were published that same year. However, for some reason, perhaps because he was viewed by New York critics as a "modern" composer of serious works, Griffes insisted that the compositions be published under the pseudonym, Arthur Tomlinson. He even instructed his family not to tell anyone that *he* was "Arthur Tomlinson."

Sometime in 1918 or 1919 Griffes wrote two more sets of children's pieces, *Six Familiar Songs* (for treble clef) and *Six Pieces for Treble Clef*. These were sold to Schirmer in June 1919 for $110.00 (comparable to about $900.00 in 1994), and published in 1920, the year of Griffes' death.

According to Griffes' sister, Marguerite, G. Schirmer sent some of the Arthur Tomlinson pieces to Griffes' former piano teacher in Elmira, Mary Selena Broughton. Miss Broughton did not recognize the pseudonym, did not like the pieces, and sent them back to Schirmer. She later told Griffes about the incident and he "roared with laughter" but did not tell Miss Broughton that he was Arthur Tomlinson nor why he was laughing. Miss Broughton did not find out why Charles had been so amused until a visit with Griffes' mother and Marguerite, some time after the composer's death. One wonders how anyone could have missed the connection between "Arthur Tomlinson" and Griffes—Tomlinson was his mother's maiden name (and Griffes' middle name) and Arthur was the name of his brother. In any case, Griffes' charming children's pieces are a welcome addition to the literature.

—DONNA K. ANDERSON
SUNY College at Cortland

CONTENTS

SIX SHORT PIECES

1
March

Charles T. Griffes
(Arthur Tomlinson)

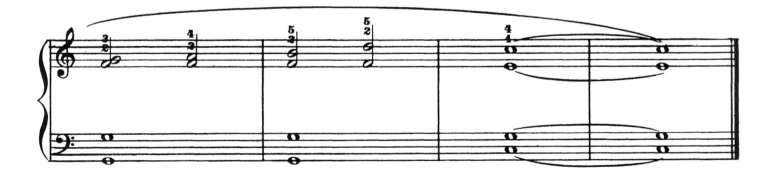

2
Dance Song

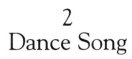

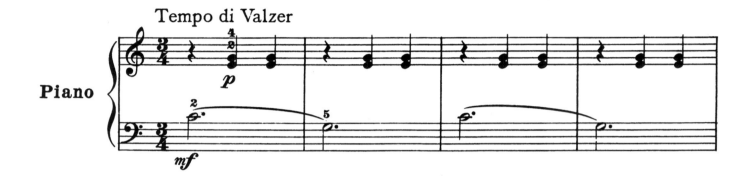

3
Marching Song

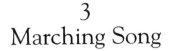

Piano

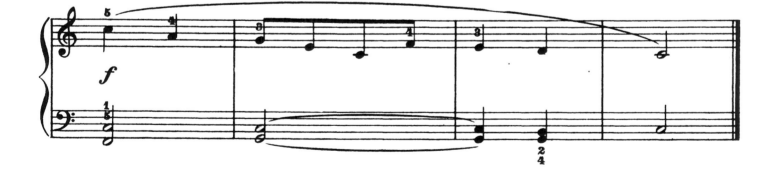

4
Evening Song

Piano

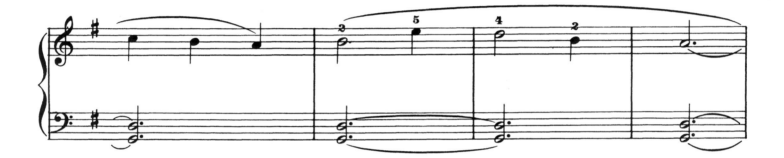

5
Parade March

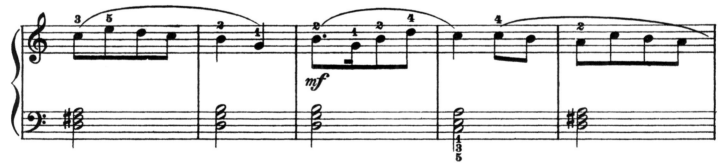

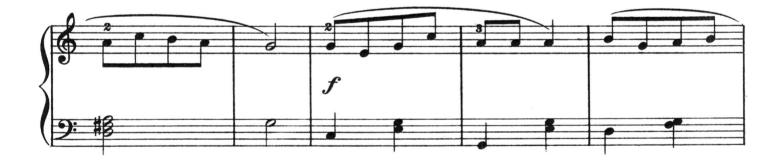

6
Waltz

Piano

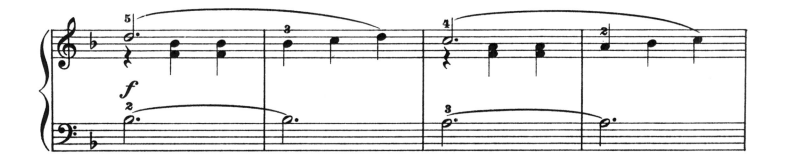

SIX BUGLE-CALL PIECES

1
Reveille

2
Taps

In slow time

3
Adjutant's Call

4
The General's March

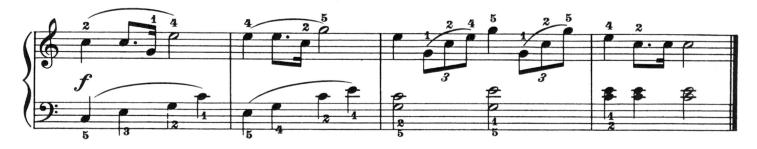

5
Assembly March

Moderato

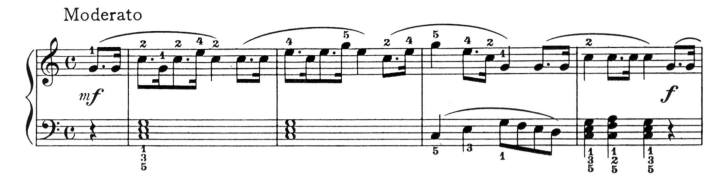

6
To The Colors

In quick time

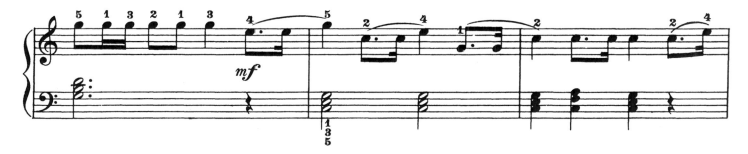

SIX PATRIOTIC SONGS

1
America

2
Yankee Doodle

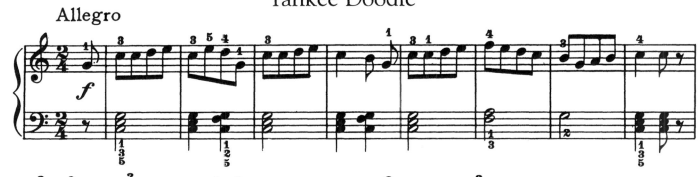

3
Marching Through Georgia

In marching time

4
The Star-Spangled Banner

Allegro maestoso

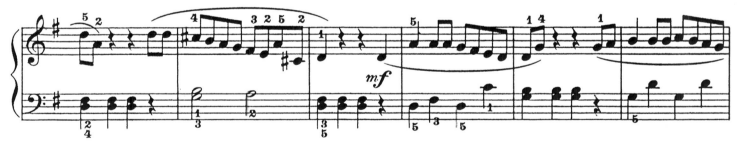

5
The Red, White and Blue

In marching time

6
Dixie

Allegro

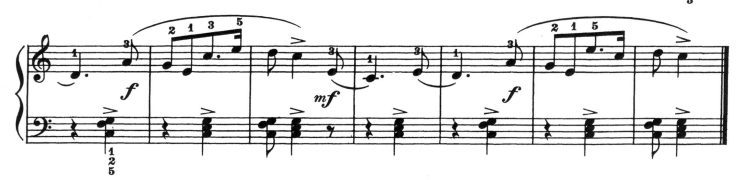

SIX FAMILIAR SONGS

1
My Old Kentucky Home

2
Old Folks At Home

3
America

Andante

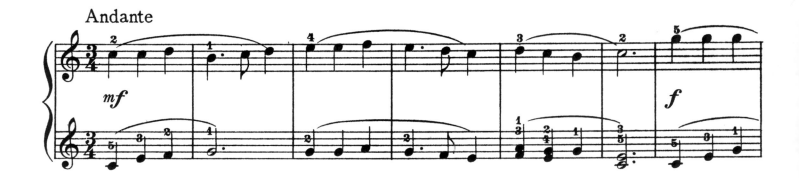

4
Yankee Doodle

Allegro

5
Maryland, My Maryland

6
The Old Oaken Bucket

SIX PIECES FOR TREBLE CLEF

1

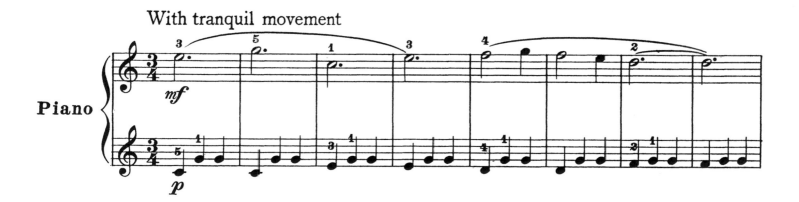

2

3

Like a Waltz

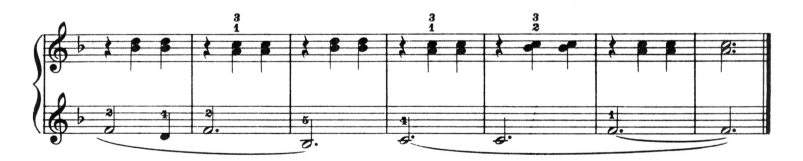

4

Quick and spirited

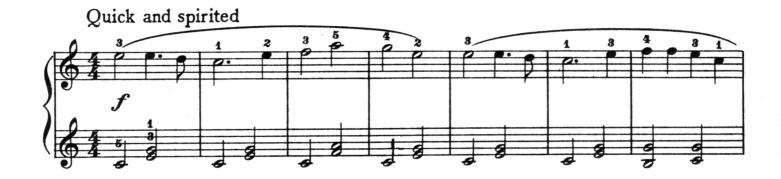

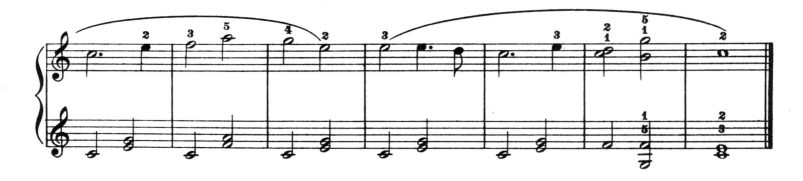

5

6

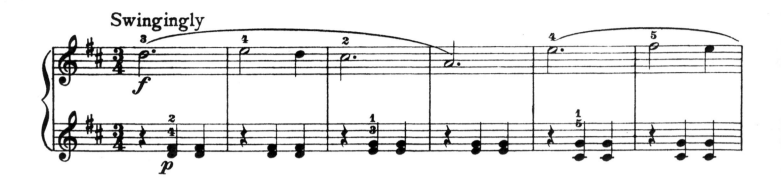

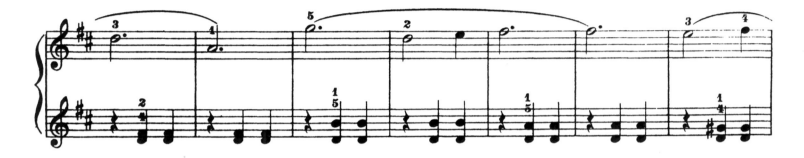